Bulletin Boards for Busy Hands

Anita Reith Stohs

Illustrated by Bill Clark

CPH™
SAINT LOUIS

To Joshua and Rebecca Box

2 Timothy 3:14–15

Copyright © 1995 Concordia Publishing House
3558 S. Jefferson Avenue, St. Louis, MO 63118-3968
Manufactured in the United States of America

1   2   3   4   5   6   7   8   9   10   04   03   02   01   00   99   98   97   96   95

Table of Contents

A Note to Teachers

These bulletin board ideas are really interactive projects. They involve children in Christian early childhood programs in making Bible-based displays. The teacher provides the background and lettering; the children complete an age-appropriate art or craft activity that is an integral part of the bulletin board. Where necessary, patterns are provided. You can enlarge them on an overhead projector to meet your needs.

You'll also find suggestions for alternative ways to make each bulletin board. Adapt these activities to the abilities of your class and the art materials you have. Many of the bulletin boards also can be adapted to reinforce other Bible stories. Be creative, and encourage your students to be creative as well.

Children learn by doing. As they plan, make, and look at a bulletin board about a specific Bible story, they will be more likely to remember the story and its meaning. After the bulletin board is taken down, send home the individual pictures or craft objects as ongoing reminders of the Bible story.

While this book's emphasis is classroom bulletin boards, the ideas can be easily adapted to posters or other individual projects.

Bulletin Board Guidelines

BACKGROUND MATERIALS

Experiment with different textures and materials:

Aluminum foil
Bible-story leaflets
Bond paper
Burlap
Cardboard
Construction paper
Fabric
Maps
Netting
Newspaper
Newsprint
Paper doilies
Poster board
Poster paper
Styrofoam pieces
Tissue paper
Wallpaper
Wrapping paper

BORDERS

Borders can be purchased at a local teacher supply store. You also can make borders from easy-to-find materials such as these:

Crepe paper
Paper chains
Paper strips
Plastic tape
Ribbon
Sponge prints
Stickers
Styrofoam pieces

Vegetable prints
Wallpaper borders
Yarn

When cutting borders from strips of paper, place several long strips together. Either cut the strips straight or accordion-fold them before cutting. Use Christian symbols that reinforce Bible stories or themes, for example, hearts for love, crosses for Lent, butterflies for Easter, or stars for Epiphany.

LETTERS

Letters may be cut, drawn, or outlined in many creative ways. For your convenience, an alphabet has been provided on pages 61–62.

- Cut letters from the materials suggested for the bulletin board backgrounds.

- Draw letters with crayons, markers, tempera paint, colored glue, chalk dipped in sugar water, or glitter pens. Experiment with the unusual effects that can be made with special markers or crayons.

- Outline letters with ribbon, yarn, toothpicks, pipe cleaners, straws, sticks, sequins, glitter, small pieces of paper, or pasta.

ENLARGING PATTERNS

In addition to the patterns provided, you can find pattern ideas in old Sunday school leaflets or curriculum materials. Use an overhead projector to enlarge patterns when necessary.

- Trace your design on a piece of acetate.

- Project the design on a piece of paper taped to the wall.

- Trace the design on the paper and cut it out. Draw in details or let the children fill the shape with drawings, paintings, printing, or collage materials.

ATTACHING MATERIALS

Paper and fabric can be stapled to the bulletin board. You may need to use push pins or thumbtacks to secure heavier objects. Push pins and thumbtacks also can be used to suspend hanging objects from the top of the bulletin board. Use glue to attach paper and other light-weight objects to the background.

Assemble the board yourself or supervise the students closely as they use staplers, push pins, or thumbtacks to attach their projects.

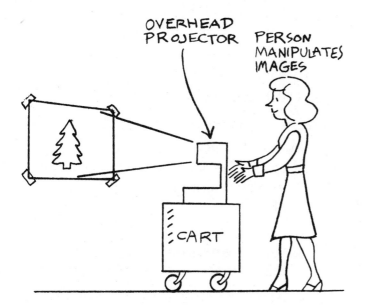

OVERHEAD PROJECTOR   PERSON MANIPULATES IMAGES

CART

See What God Made

BIBLE STORY

Creation (Genesis 1)

MATERIALS

Poster paper
Cardboard
Pencil
Nature objects in a box
Craft glue
Ziplock plastic bags
Push pins

TEACHER TASKS

1. Discuss the things God made to fill the earth. Explain that God's creation can be seen every day in the world of nature.

2. If possible, lead the children on a nature walk. Gather grasses, rocks, nuts, feathers, sticks, pine cones, or other objects to use for the bulletin board. You also can gather the objects yourself. Place them in a box.

3. Cover the bulletin board with poster paper.

4. Cut a strip of cardboard the length of the bulletin board. Lightly outline the letters "See What God Made" with a pencil. Place the cardboard on a work table.

5. Give a ziplock bag to each child.

6. Attach the completed cardboard banner and filled bags to the bulletin board with push pins.

STUDENT TASKS

1. Fill in or outline the letters with small nature objects.

2. Choose a nature object to put in your ziplock bag.

OTHER IDEAS

1. Use poster board instead of cardboard.

2. Cut different colors of poster paper into strips for grass, mountains, and sky.

3. Glue or tie nature objects to yarn. Hang them from the top of the bulletin board.

4. Allow the children to change the contents of the bags.

Touch What God Made

BIBLE STORY

Creation (Genesis 1)

MATERIALS

Construction paper
Scissors
Clear self-adhesive paper
Lightweight nature objects in a box

TEACHER TASKS

1. If possible, take a nature walk with your children and gather lightweight nature objects. Place the box in the classroom. Encourage the children to touch the objects and describe how they feel — for example, rough, smooth, or fuzzy.

2. Cut letters from construction paper for the words "Touch What God Made." Attach them to the bulletin board.

3. Cover the bulletin board with clear self-adhesive paper, sticky side out. Attach it so the children can easily reach it.

4. Lead the class in a thank-You prayer for the sense of touch God has given us and the different things He made for us to feel.

5. While the bulletin board is displayed, encourage the children to touch and compare the objects.

STUDENT TASKS

Pick a nature object from the box. Stick it to the self-adhesive paper.

OTHER IDEAS

1. Encourage the children to add other nature items to the bulletin board.

2. Use burlap or poster paper for the background.

Praise God for All Creation

BIBLE STORY

Creation (Genesis 1; Psalm 148)

MATERIALS

Blue poster paper
Markers or crayons
Pencil (*optional*)
String (*optional*)

TEACHER TASKS

1. Cut blue poster paper to cover the bulletin board. Place it on a work table.

2. Write "Praise God for All Creation" on the paper.

3. Draw a large circle in the center of the paper. (To draw the circle, tie a string around a pencil. Hold the end of the string in the center of the area you want the circle. Draw the circle with the pencil by keeping the string taut.)

4. Set out markers or crayons.

5. Read Psalm 148 to the children.

6. Attach the poster paper to the bulletin board.

STUDENT TASKS

1. Listen to Psalm 148. Pick a part of creation you would like to praise God for making.

2. Use markers or crayons to draw your choice around or inside the circle on the poster paper.

3. Praise God for the parts of creation on the bulletin board.

OTHER IDEAS

1. Use tempera paint or torn paper to make the illustrations.

2. Cut the circle from blue poster paper.

God Keeps His Promises

BIBLE STORY

The Great Flood (Genesis 6:1–9:17)

MATERIALS

Light-blue poster paper
Masking tape
Construction paper
Scissors
Prism (*optional*)
Markers or crayons

TEACHER TASKS

1. Cut light-blue poster paper to cover the bulletin board. Tape it to a wall.
2. Enlarge the patterns on page 12. Trace the shapes directly on the light-blue poster paper. Place the poster paper on a work table.
3. Cut letters from construction paper for the words "God Keeps His Promises." Attach them to the poster paper.
4. Set out construction paper and scissors.
5. Explain the colors in a rainbow: red, orange, yellow, green, blue, indigo, violet. (If possible, use a prism to show how light separates into these colors.)
6. Ask the children to tell about the dove and rainbow in the story. Emphasize that just as God kept His promises to Noah, He keeps His promises to us. Discuss the ways God keeps His promises to us.
7. Attach the poster paper to the bulletin board.

STUDENT TASKS

1. Cut or tear pieces of construction paper for the rainbow and dove.
2. Glue the pieces inside the figures.

OTHER IDEAS

1. Use sponges to stamp the rainbow and dove with tempera paint.
2. Color the rainbow and dove with markers or crayons.
3. Trace the patterns on white paper. Cut them out and glue them to the backround paper.
4. Use pieces of yarn or crepe paper to make the rainbow.

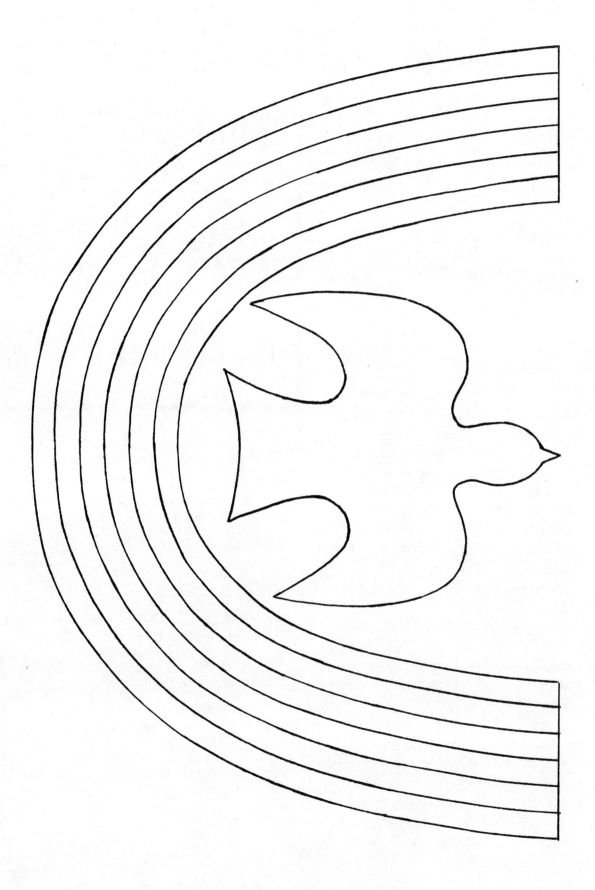

God's Children Forgive

BIBLE STORY

Jacob and Esau Meet Again
(Genesis 33:1–4)

MATERIALS

White poster paper
Markers or crayons
Pencil (*optional*)

TEACHER TASKS

1. Cut white poster paper to cover the bulletin board. Place it on a work table.

2. Write "God's Children Forgive" on the paper.

3. Discuss Jacob and Esau's reunion. Emphasize the importance of forgiveness. Remind the children that we forgive others because God forgave us. Tell them sometimes people shake hands to show they have forgiven each other and are friends again.

4. Help young children trace around their hands.

5. Attach the poster paper to the bulletin board.

STUDENT TASKS

1. Place your hand on the poster paper. Trace around it.

2. Place your other hand partly over the first handprint. Trace around it.

3. Tell about a time you forgave someone else or were forgiven.

OTHER IDEAS

1. Cut handprints from flesh-colored construction paper.

2. Find other Bible stories in which one person forgives another. Write the names of each pair on a set of shaking hands.

God Intended It for Good

BIBLE STORY

The Life of Joseph (Genesis 37, 39–50)

MATERIALS

Fabric
Construction paper
Scissors
White paper
Fine-point markers
Photo album pages

TEACHER TASKS

1. Cover the bulletin board with fabric. (A striped pattern, like Joseph's brightly colored coat, would be appropriate.)

2. Cut letters from construction paper for the words "God Intended It for Good: The Life of Joseph." Attach them to the bulletin board.

3. Cut white paper to fit the photo album pages.

4. Set out fine-point markers.

5. Review the life of Joseph with the children. Ask what Joseph meant when he said, "God intended it for good" (Genesis 50:20).

STUDENT TASKS

1. Use markers to draw a picture of an event in Joseph's life.

2. Work together to put the pictures in order. Put one picture in each album page.

3. Help your teacher attach the album pages to the bulletin board.

OTHER IDEAS

1. Assign an event in Joseph's life to each child.

2. Use crayons or colored pencils.

3. For older students: Think about a time when something happened in your life that you thought was bad but it ended up being good. Draw a picture of it.

4. Use this bulletin board to illustrate other Bible stories with an easy-to-identify sequence of events.

God Was with Moses

BIBLE STORY

The Birth of Moses (Exodus 2:1–10)

MATERIALS

Light-blue poster paper
Markers
Yellow construction paper
Scissors
White poster board
Macaroni
Craft glue
Fabric scraps
Green ribbon

TEACHER TASKS

1. Cover the bulletin board with light-blue poster paper.

2. Draw wavy blue lines across the paper to represent water.

3. Cut letters from yellow construction paper for the words "God Was with Moses." Attach them to the bulletin board.

4. Enlarge the pattern on page 16 and trace it directly onto white poster board. Use a marker to add details.

5. Cut fabric scraps into small pieces.

6. Cut varying lengths of green ribbon.

7. Discuss how God was with Moses in his basket and how He is with us wherever we are today.

8. Attach Moses in his basket to the bulletin board.

9. Lead the children in the following song (to the tune of "Mary Had a Little Lamb").

Moses floated on the Nile, on the Nile, on the Nile.
Moses floated on the Nile—
God was with him there.

Anytime and anywhere, anywhere, anywhere.
Anytime and anywhere—
God is with me there.

STUDENT TASKS

1. Glue the macaroni onto the basket.

2. Glue the fabric squares onto the blanket.

3. Draw Moses' face.

4. Glue green ribbon for reeds onto the poster paper.

5. Talk about some of the places where God is with you.

OTHER IDEAS

1. Use markers to draw the letters.

2. Cut the letters from fabric or use pieces of ribbon to make them.

3. Use real grass or reeds instead of ribbon.

4. Use green plastic tape instead of ribbon.

5. Use blue yarn to make the waves.

6. Use crayons to rub a textured pattern on the basket.

Pattern for "God Was with Moses"

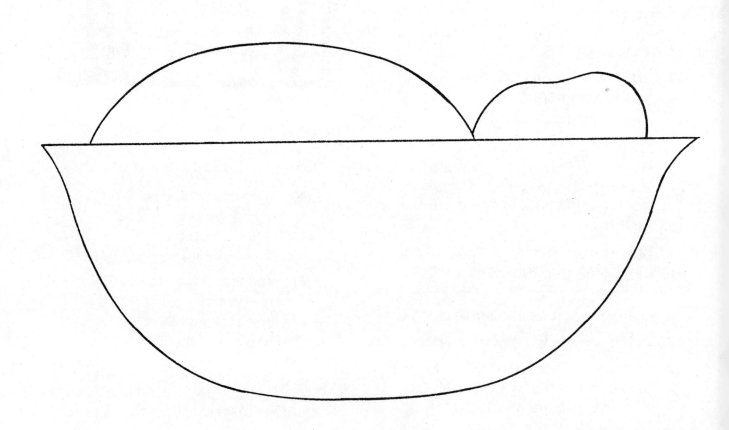

God's Helpers Today

BIBLE STORY

The Call of Moses (Exodus 3:1–4:17)

MATERIALS

White poster paper
Wallpaper
Scissors
Flesh-colored construction paper
Craft glue
Movable eyes
Orange, yellow, black, and brown
    yarn
Markers or crayons

TEACHER TASKS

1. Cover the bulletin board with white poster paper.

2. Cut letters from wallpaper for the words "God's Helpers Today." Attach them to the bulletin board.

3. Enlarge the pattern on page 18. Use it to cut a head and neck from flesh-colored construction paper for each child. Use just the upper-body section to cut "shirts" from different patterns of wallpaper.

4. Cut yarn into 12″ pieces.

5. Set out craft glue, movable eyes, scissors, and markers or crayons.

6. Discuss God's call for Moses to be His special helper. Tell the children that God has chosen us to be His helpers too.

7. Help the students attach their self-portraits to the bulletin board and write their names beside them.

STUDENT TASKS

1. Choose a wallpaper "shirt" and glue it to the head and neck section.

2. Glue on movable eyes and yarn hair. (Trim the yarn as needed.)

3. Cut a mouth and a nose from construction paper and glue them onto the face.

4. Glue your self-portrait to the poster paper and write your name under it.

5. Take turns telling how you can be God's helper.

OTHER IDEAS

1. Make 3-D facial features. Fold a piece of construction paper in half and trace the outline of a nose and mouth along the fold. Cut them out. Glue the edges of the nose and mouth on the paper so the center fold sticks out from the face.

2. Draw hair and facial features with markers or crayons or cut them from construction paper.

3. Cut the head and neck section from construction paper, wrapping paper, or fabric.

4. Write the name on the upper-body section.

The Lord Is My Strength

BIBLE STORY

The Crossing of the Red Sea
(Exodus 13:17–15:21)

MATERIALS

> Light-blue, dark-blue, and yellow
>   poster paper
> Markers
> Scissors
> Pipe cleaners
> Stapler

TEACHER TASKS

1. Cover the top third of the bulletin board with light-blue poster paper. Write "The Lord Is My Strength" across the top of the paper with markers.

2. Cut a line of waves along the top of the dark-blue poster paper. Cover the middle third of the bulletin board by overlapping the dark blue on the light-blue poster paper.

3. Cover the bottom third of the bulletin board with yellow poster paper.

4. Cut pipe cleaners into different lengths. Show how to make people shapes from pipe cleaners.

5. Tell the children that after God saved the Israelites by parting the Red Sea, Moses sang in praise, "The Lord is my strength."

6. Staple the pipe-cleaner figures along the bottom of the bulletin board.

STUDENT TASKS

1. Make people shapes out of pipe cleaners.

2. Tell of a way that our strong God protects you today.

OTHER IDEAS

1. Draw people with markers or use yarn.

2. Cut circles and triangles from construction paper. Put them together to make a row of people.

Sing to the Lord

BIBLE STORY

The Songs of Moses and Miriam
(Exodus 15:1–21)

MATERIALS

White poster paper
Markers
Black plastic tape
Brightly colored adhesive stickers
Rhythm instruments
Songbook

TEACHER TASKS

1. Cut white poster paper to cover the bulletin board. Place it on a work table.

2. Write "Sing to the Lord" across the top of the paper with markers.

3. Use black plastic tape to make one or more sets of five parallel lines across the poster paper. If desired, add treble and bass clefs.

4. Set out brightly colored adhesive stickers and rhythm instruments.

5. Tell the children about the songs Moses and Miriam sang to praise God. Discuss the way we write music today. Show an example from a songbook.

6. Attach the paper to the bulletin board.

STUDENT TASKS

1. Place brightly colored adhesive stickers on the poster paper. (There is no "correct" place to put the dots.)

2. "Read" the notes as you clap or use rhythm instruments to accompany familiar songs of praise.

OTHER IDEAS

1. Cut notes from black construction paper.

2. Use a cardboard tube dipped in tempera paint to stamp notes on the paper.

3. Draw the music lines with a marker or crayon.

O Give Thanks

BIBLE STORY

God Sends Manna and Quail to Feed His People (Exodus 16)

MATERIALS

Paper or plastic checked table-
     cloth
Construction paper
Scissors
Pizza cardboards
Glue
Stick pins

TEACHER TASKS

1. Cover the bulletin board with the tablecloth.

2. Cut letters from construction paper for the words "O Give Thanks for Pizza." Attach them to the bulletin board.

3. For each pizza, cut a yellow circle for the crust and a smaller red circle for the tomato sauce. The yellow circle should be slightly smaller than the pizza cardboard.

4. Set out construction paper, glue, scissors, and pencils.

5. Describe how God fed the Israelites in the desert with manna and quail.

6. Divide the children into small groups. Give each group a pizza cardboard, a yellow circle, and a red circle.

7. Attach the pizzas to the bulletin board with stick pins.

STUDENT TASKS

1. In your group, glue the yellow and red circles onto the pizza cardboard.

2. Cut construction paper to make mushrooms, cheese, pepperoni, or other toppings.

3. Glue the toppings onto the pizza

OTHER IDEAS

1. Use a circle cut from construction paper instead of a pizza cardboard.

2. Cut one large circle as a pizza for all the children to "top."

3. Outline "Praise God for Pizza" with topping pieces.

4. Use markers or crayons to draw the tablecloth pattern.

On Their Way

BIBLE STORY

The Israelites Travel to Canaan
(Exodus through Deuteronomy)

MATERIALS

Burlap
Bible story leaflets about the
    Exodus
Scissors
Styrofoam trays
Glue
Yarn
Hole punch
Stick pins

TEACHER TASKS

1. Cover the bulletin board with burlap.
2. Cut letters from colorful sections of Bible story leaflets for the words "On Their Way: The Israelites' Wilderness Wandering." Attach them to the bulletin board.
3. Trim Bible story leaflet pictures to fit inside Styrofoam trays.
4. Cut pieces of yarn that will fit around the Styrofoam trays.
5. Cut a 6" piece of yarn for each tray. For younger children, tie the yarn through the hole.
6. Set out craft glue, scissors, and hole punch.
7. Tell the children about the 40 years the Israelites wandered in the wilderness. Emphasize the ways God helped and protected them.
8. Attach the plaques to the bulletin board with stick pins.

STUDENT TASKS

1. Choose a Bible story picture. Glue it inside the Styrofoam tray.
2. Glue yarn around the edge of the tray for a frame. Trim excess yarn.
3. Punch a hole in the top of your picture. Tie a piece of yarn through the hole for a hanger.
4. As you hang your picture, tell the story that goes with it.

OTHER IDEAS

1. Punch holes around the sides of the Styrofoam tray. Use yarn to stitch through the holes.
2. Tape plastic wrap over the tray for "glass."
3. Move the appropriate picture to the top of the bulletin board as you study that story in the Exodus unit.

We Help One Another

BIBLE STORY

The Story of Ruth (Ruth)

MATERIALS

Light-colored poster paper
Scissors
Markers or crayons

TEACHER TASKS

1. Cut poster paper to cover the bulletin board. Place it on a work table.

2. Write "We Help One Another" across the poster paper with markers or crayons.

3. Set out markers or crayons for the students to use.

4. Talk about the different ways Ruth was a helper to Naomi.

5. Attach the poster paper to the bulletin board.

STUDENT TASKS

1. Trace around your hand with a crayon or marker.

2. Draw a picture of something in your hand that you can use to help others.

OTHER IDEAS

1. Cut handprints and tools from construction paper.

2. Trace the outlines of real objects used to help others.

3. Fill in the hands and tools with crayons, markers, or torn pieces of construction paper.

4. Fasten lightweight pictures, boxes, or objects to the handprints.

5. Use tempera paint and stamp handprints onto the poster paper.

God Sends the Rain

BIBLE REFERENCE

God Gives Us Rain (Psalm 147:8)

MATERIALS

Blue and white poster paper
Scissors
Cotton balls
Glue
String
Waxed paper
Tape

TEACHER TASKS

1. Cover the bulletin board with blue poster paper.

2. Cut letters from white poster paper for the words "God Sends the Rain." Attach them to the bulletin board.

3. Enlarge the pattern on page 25 and trace it directly onto a piece of white poster paper. Cut out the cloud. Place it on a work table.

4. Cut string for rain. Cut strips of waxed paper the length of the string.

5. Set out glue, cotton balls, and tape.

6. Read Psalm 147:8. Lead the children in a prayer of thanksgiving for the rain God sends.

7. Attach the cloud to the blue poster paper.

STUDENT TASKS

1. Glue cotton balls onto the cloud.

2. Lay the strings on waxed paper and dot glue along them to make raindrops. Let the glue dry.

3. Carefully pull the strings away from the waxed paper. Tape them along the bottom of the back of the cloud.

OTHER IDEAS

1. Cut a strip of green poster paper to cover the bottom few inches of the bulletin board. Fringe the paper to make grass to illustrate the last section of Psalm 147:8.

2. Add glitter to the glue.

3. Let the children glue cotton balls onto the blue poster paper to make their own cloud shapes.

4. Use glitter, yarn, or tinsel to make rain.

5. Read Psalm 147:16–17. Add other forms of precipitation.

6. Cut the cloud from poster board. Punch a hole in the top and hang it from the top of the bulletin board.

7. Use this bulletin board for the story of Elijah and the prophets of Baal.

Pattern for "God Sends the Rain"

I Have Called You by Name

BIBLE REFERENCE

God Summons Us by Name
(Isaiah 43:1)

MATERIALS

Colorful poster paper
Markers
Construction paper
Scissors
Assorted decorative objects (buttons, sequins, ribbon, etc.)
Craft glue

TEACHER TASKS

1. Cut poster paper to cover the bulletin board. Place it on a work table.

2. Write "I Have Called You by Name—You Are Mine" across the poster paper.

3. Cut a large letter from construction paper for the first letter of each child's name.

4. Set out decorative objects, scissors, and craft glue.

5. Remind the children that they are all special to God. He has called us to be His children and He knows our names. Read the last part of Isaiah 43:1. Ask the children how this makes them feel.

6. Attach the poster paper with letters to the bulletin board.

STUDENT TASKS

1. Glue decorative objects onto your initial letter.

2. Glue the letter to the poster paper.

3. Write the rest of your name after the letter with a marker.

OTHER IDEAS

1. Trace the letters onto poster paper and let the children use markers, crayons, or tempera paint to color them.

2. Decorate letters with stickers or small pieces of construction paper.

Only God Can Save

BIBLE STORY

Daniel in the Lions' Den (Daniel 6)

MATERIALS

Poster paper
Yellow, black, and flesh-colored
    construction paper
Scissors
Plate
Glue
Markers or crayons

TEACHER TASKS

1. Cover the bulletin board with poster paper.

2. Cut letters from construction paper for the words "Only God Can Save." Attach them to the poster paper.

3. Use a plate to trace a circle on yellow construction paper for each child.

4. Trace a circle on flesh-colored construction paper for Daniel's face.

5. Cut triangles from black construction paper for a nose for each child. Cut two half-circles from yellow construction paper for ears for each child. Cut strips of black paper for Daniel's hair.

6. Set out scissors, glue, and markers or crayons.

7. Review how God saved Daniel from the lions. Emphasize that God saved Daniel from the lions, and He saves us from dangers too.

8. Put Daniel in the center of the bulletin board. Attach the lions around him.

STUDENT TASKS

1. Glue the black triangle in the center of the yellow circle to make a nose.

2. Use markers or crayons to draw the lion's eyes and mouth.

3. Use a scissors to cut a fringe around the circle for the lion's mane. Glue on the yellow half-circles for ears.

4. Work together to draw Daniel's face and glue on his hair and beard.

OTHER IDEAS

1. Make a face for the angel.

2. Glue on pieces of construction paper or yarn for the lion's mane.

3. Use circle stickers for eyes.

Oh, Come, Emmanuel

BIBLE STORY

The Annunciation (Luke 1:26–38)

MATERIALS

Red Christmas wrapping paper
Glitter pen or crayons
Green poster paper
Construction paper
Scissors
Religious Christmas cards
Double-stick tape
Waxed paper
Glue
Decorative Christmas stickers

TEACHER TASKS

1. Cover the bulletin board with red Christmas wrapping paper.

2. Write "Oh, Come, Emmanuel" across the bulletin board with a glitter pen or crayon.

3. Enlarge the tree pattern on page 29 and trace it directly onto green poster paper. Cut out the tree and place it on a work table.

4. Cut 25 rectangles from construction paper. Number them 1–25.

5. Cut strips of double-stick tape; place them on waxed paper.

6. Set out scissors, glue, and stickers.

7. Ask the children what they think Mary had to do to get ready for Jesus' birth.

8. Help the children arrange the Christmas cards in a sequence that reflects the events of Jesus' birth. Place a numbered rectangle with each card. Save the card with the best nativity scene for number 25.

9. Attach the tree to the bulletin board.

STUDENT TASKS

1. Fasten the top part of each numbered paper to the top of a Christmas card with double-stick tape. Glue the back of the card to the tree. Put number 25 on the top of the tree.

2. Use self-adhesive stickers to decorate the rest of the tree.

3. On each day of December, remove the number that corresponds with the date. As you do, tell what the picture below it shows.

OTHER IDEAS

1. Decorate the tree with metallic stickers or snowflakes.

2. Add fabric trim, glitter, or yarn to the tree.

3. Cut the last card and its cover in a star pattern.

4. Cut "Oh, Come, Emmanuel" from metallic gift wrap.

5. Cut "Oh, Come, Emmanuel" from colorful Christmas cards.

6. Cut the cards and covers in circle shapes.

Pattern for "Oh, Come, Emmanuel"

Away in a Manger

BIBLE STORY

Jesus Is Born (Luke 2:1–7)

MATERIALS

Blue poster paper
Pink and yellow construction paper
Scissors
White poster board
Markers
Craft glue
Fabric scraps
Masking tape
Waxed paper
Straw

TEACHER TASKS

1. Cover the bulletin board with blue poster paper.

2. Cut letters from yellow construction paper for the words "Away in a Manger." Attach them to the bulletin board.

3. Enlarge the pattern on page 31 and trace it directly onto the white poster board. Use a black marker to trace it. Cut it out.

4. Cut a piece of pink construction paper to fit the baby's head. Glue it in place.

5. Cut fabric into small pieces (2″ or 3″ squares). Cut straw into 6″ pieces.

6. Cut squares of waxed paper. Cut masking tape into 3″ or 4″ pieces. Place them on waxed paper.

7. Set out craft glue, markers, and scissors.

8. Discuss the birth of Jesus. Emphasize His arrival as a baby—truly human—born to poor parents. Discuss why His first bed was a manger.

9. Attach the manger to the bulletin board.

STUDENT TASKS

1. Draw Jesus' face with markers.

2. Glue on fabric pieces for swaddling clothes.

3. Cover the manger with pieces of masking tape.

4. Glue straw pieces around Jesus' head to make a halo.

5. Glue straw inside the manger.

OTHER IDEAS

1. Cut Jesus' face from fabric.

2. Cut facial features from fabric or construction paper.

3. Glue on tinsel or a metallic garland for the halo.

4. Add self-adhesive metallic stars to the sky. Draw stars with a glitter pen.

5. Substitute yellow Easter grass for straw.

6. Draw the halo and title with a glitter pen.

7. Cover the bulletin board with burlap or Christmas fabric.

8. Duplicate the pattern below for each child. Let the children color the picture or glue on pieces of paper.

Glue the picture onto a firm backing and add fabric or straw. Encourage them to add star stickers at home for each day of Advent.

9. Cover the bulletin board with Christmas gift wrap. Add a ribbon cross. Place the manger pattern in the center of the cross. Emphasize Jesus' birth as part of God's plan to save His people from their sins.

10. Use this bulletin board as an Advent calendar. Cut the pattern apart so that Jesus and the manger are two sections. Put up only the manger. Have the children add a star to the bulletin board each day before Christmas. On Christmas Day, add baby Jesus to the manger.

Pattern for "Away in a Manger"

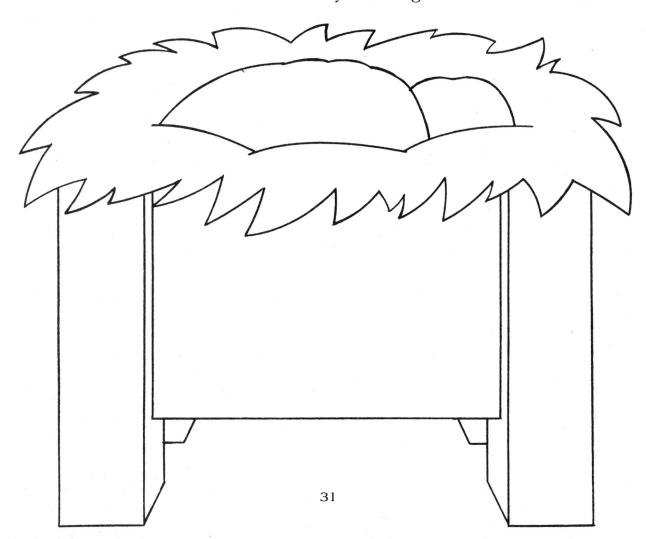

31

Joy to the World

BIBLE STORY

The Angels Appear to the Shepherds
(Luke 2:8–20)

MATERIALS

Dark-blue poster paper
Metallic wrapping paper
Scissors
White paper doilies
Sequins or other decorative trim
Craft glue
Self-adhesive stars

TEACHER TASKS

1. Cover the bulletin board with dark-blue poster paper.

2. Cut letters from metallic wrapping paper for the words "Joy to the World." Attach them to the bulletin board.

3. Enlarge the pattern on page 31 and trace it directly onto metallic wrapping paper. Cut it out. Attach it to the bulletin board.

4. Duplicate the angel pattern on page 33 for each child.

5. Cut paper doilies into small pieces.

6. Set out craft glue and decorative trim.

7. Tell how the angels announced Jesus' birth to the shepherds. Emphasize that Jesus is our Savior too.

8. Help the children attach their angels to the bulletin board.

STUDENT TASKS

1. Cut out the angel pattern and trace it onto metallic wrapping paper.

2. Glue pieces of doily lace and other decorative trim on the angel.

3. Stick self-adhesive stars onto the poster paper.

OTHER IDEAS

1. Make wings for the angels by dipping the children's hands in tempera paint and stamping the wings.

2. Cut lettering, stars, and the manger from construction paper and add glitter.

3. Add lace and decorative trim to the letters and manger.

4. Omit the manger and cut a stable or Bethlehem skyline instead.

5. Omit the manger and add the shepherds in their fields.

6. Cut angels from metallic paper doilies.

7. Hang the angels from the top of the bulletin board.

Pattern for "Joy to the World"

Happy Birthday, Jesus

BIBLE STORY

The Shepherds Praise God for Jesus
(Luke 2:20)

MATERIALS

Birthday wrapping paper
Brightly colored construction paper
Scissors
Pencil (*optional*)
Hole punch
Curling ribbon

TEACHER TASKS

1. Cover the bulletin board with birthday wrapping paper.

2. Cut construction-paper letters for the words "Happy Birthday, Jesus." Attach them to the bulletin board.

3. Cut geometric shapes (circles, triangles, and squares) from construction paper. If needed, lightly pencil in lines for the children to cut along.

4. Cut curling ribbon into different lengths. Curl some of it and hang it from the top of the bulletin board.

5. Set out scissors and a hole punch.

6. Ask the children what they think it would have been like to be one of the shepherds who saw Jesus. Emphasize the joy we have because He came as our Savior.

7. Show how to cut a spring.

8. Hang completed springs from the top of the bulletin board.

STUDENT TASKS

1. Cut around the construction-paper shapes all the way to their centers.

2. Punch a hole in the center of the shape.

3. Tie a piece of curling ribbon through the hole.

OTHER IDEAS

1. Cut springs from metallic paper.

2. Hang tinsel and Christmas ornaments from the top of the bulletin board.

3. Tie springs with short pieces of ribbon. Tape them to the bulletin board.

Come and Worship

BIBLE STORY

The Wise Men Visit Jesus (Matthew 2:1–12)

MATERIALS

Dark-blue poster paper
Yellow construction paper
Scissors
Craft sticks
Craft glue
Glitter
Cardboard
Self-adhesive stars
String

TEACHER TASKS

1. Cut dark-blue poster paper to cover the bulletin board. Place it on a work table.

2. Cut yellow construction-paper letters for the words "Come and Worship." Attach them to the poster paper.

3. Glue together six or more craft sticks to form a star. Cut string for hanging the star when finished.

4. Cut a rectangular-shaped house from cardboard.

5. Set out craft glue, glitter, craft sticks, and self-adhesive stars.

6. Tell the children how the Wise Men followed the star to the place where Jesus was. Ask the children to identify the gifts they brought. Emphasize that Jesus was worshiped as King.

7. Help the children add glue and glitter to the craft-stick star.

8. Attach the dark-blue poster paper to the bulletin board. Attach the house. Hang the star from the top of the bulletin board.

STUDENT TASKS

1. Add glue and glitter to the star.

2. Glue craft sticks onto the cardboard house.

3. Stick self-adhesive stars onto the blue poster paper.

OTHER IDEAS

1. Add stars with glitter or crayons.

2. Dip a star-shaped cookie cutter, sponge, or an apple cut in half in tempera paint and then stamp stars on the poster paper.

3. Make one large star from large craft sticks. Allow each child to make smaller stars from smaller sticks.

4. Use notched craft sticks to make the star and house.

5. Trace a house on a piece of construction paper and use markers or crayons to draw a picture of the Wise Men worshiping Jesus.

6. Explain to the children that Jesus was older when the Wise Men visited, and He was probably living in a house.

Optional Ways to Make House

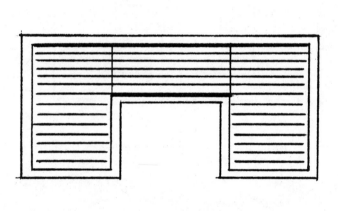

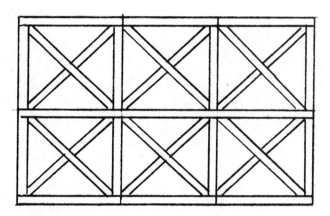

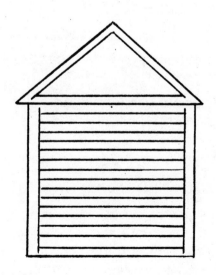

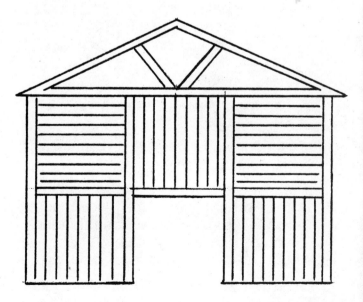

Baptized and Forgiven

BIBLE STORY

Jesus' Baptism (Matthew 3:13–17)

MATERIALS

Dark-blue poster paper
White poster board
Markers
White and light-blue construction
    paper
Scissors

TEACHER TASKS

1. Cover the bulletin board with dark-blue poster paper.

2. Enlarge the shell pattern on page 38 and trace it directly onto white poster board. Cut it out. Write "Baptized and Forgiven" on the shell. Attach it to the bulletin board.

3. Duplicate and cut out the waterdrop pattern on page 38. Enlarge if desired. Trace and cut out a light-blue waterdrop for each child.

4. Ask parents to send their child's Baptism date. If a child has not been baptized, substitute another significant date in their Christian life.

5. Set out markers.

6. Remind the children that Jesus' Baptism reminds us of our own. Emphasize that through Baptism our sins are washed away and the Holy Spirit, through the water and the Word, works the miracle of faith in our lives. Explain the symbolism of the shell and the waterdrops.

7. Attach the waterdrops to the bulletin board.

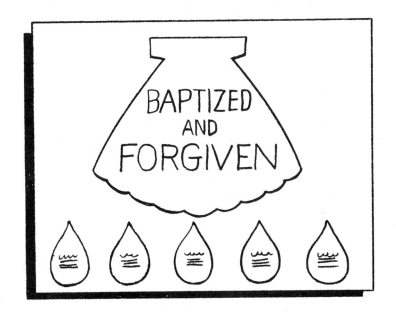

STUDENT TASKS

1. Write your name and baptismal date on your waterdrop.

2. Draw a picture of your Baptism.

OTHER IDEAS

1. Encourage children who are not baptized to draw a picture of the day when they will be baptized.

2. Write the children's names on real scallop shells. Glue them directly to the bulletin board or glue them to string and hang them from the top of the bulletin board.

3. Use a glitter pen or crayon to write the information.

4. Use a dove shape (see the pattern on page 12).

We Follow Jesus

BIBLE STORY

Jesus Calls His Disciples
(Matthew 4:18–22)

MATERIALS

Green poster paper
Construction paper
Scissors
Pencil
Markers or crayons
Glue

TEACHER TASKS

1. Cover the bulletin board with green poster paper.

2. Cut letters from construction paper for the words "We Follow Jesus." Attach them to the bulletin board.

3. Cut a large sandal from construction paper. Cut a strip of construction paper and write "Jesus" on it. Glue one end of the strip under each side of the sandal. The strip should stick above the sole like a sandal strap. Attach the "Jesus" sandal to the center, right side of the bulletin board.

4. Set out construction paper, markers or crayons, scissors, and glue.

5. Ask the children what it means to "follow the leader." Explain that Jesus is our Leader. He wants us to follow Him to our heavenly home.

6. Put the children's sandals on the board behind Jesus' sandal.

STUDENT TASKS

1. Trace your shoe on construction paper to make a sandal bottom. Cut it out.

2. Cut a strip of construction paper for your sandal. Write your name on it.

3. Glue one end of the strip under each side of the sandal.

OTHER IDEAS

1. Write "They Followed the Lord" on the bulletin board. Cut a sandal for each disciple; write his name on it. Add the names of other Bible people.

2. Cut sandals from textured wallpaper or a cork strip.

3. Draw a picture inside the sandal of something you do as you "follow Jesus."

Jesus Loves Me

BIBLE STORY

Jesus and the Children (Mark 10:13–16)

MATERIALS

Red poster paper
White construction paper
Scissors
Crayons (include crayons in skin
   tones)

TEACHER TASKS

1. Cover the bulletin board with red poster paper.
2. Cut letters from white construction paper for the words "Jesus Loves Me." Attach them to the bulletin board.
3. Duplicate the patterns on page 41. Enlarge them if needed.
4. Trace the pattern of Jesus onto white construction paper and cut it out.
5. Cut a child figure from white paper for each child.
6. Set out crayons and glue.
7. Tell the story of Jesus and the children. Emphasize His love for all people.
8. Attach the figure of Jesus to the center of the bulletin board. Attach the children's figures around Him.

STUDENT TASKS

1. Work together to color the figure of Jesus.
2. Draw yourself on your figure with markers or crayons.

OTHER IDEAS

1. Use photographs instead of figures of children. Frame them with a heart shape.
2. Cut pictures of children from magazines and catalogs to glue around Jesus.
3. Have the children draw or paint a picture of Jesus and their self-portraits.
4. Write the children's names inside the figures of children. Glue a red heart inside Jesus.
5. Paste the children's pictures inside a large heart drawn in the center of the bulletin board.
6. Take home activity: Give each child figures of Jesus and a child. When both have been colored, glue them beside each other.

Patterns for "Jesus Loves Me"

God Helps Us Grow

BIBLE STORY

God Cares for the Flowers
(Luke 12:27–28)

MATERIALS

Blue and green poster paper
Construction paper
Scissors
Glue
Markers

TEACHER TASKS

1. Cover the bulletin board with blue poster paper.

2. Cut green poster paper to cover the bottom half of the bulletin board. Fold it in half.

3. Cut one small yellow construction-paper circle for each child. Cut a large yellow construction-paper circle for the sun.

4. Set out markers and glue.

5. Write "God Helps Us Grow" inside the sun. Cut a fringe around it for rays. Attach the sun at the top center of the bulletin board.

6. Cut large circles from different colors of construction paper.

7. Cut a stem and several leaves from green construction paper for each child.

8. Read Luke 12:27–28. Ask the children how God takes care of them and helps them grow.

9. Attach the green poster paper and flowers to the bulletin board.

STUDENT TASKS

1. Take one yellow circle and one colored circle.

2. Glue the yellow circle to the center of the colored circle.

3. Fringe or cut the outside edge of the colored circle to make flower petals.

4. Draw your face inside the yellow circle.

5. Take one green stem and several leaves. Glue the leaves to the stem. Glue the stem to the flower.

6. Write your name down the stem.

7. Work together to fringe the folded side of the green poster paper.

OTHER IDEAS

1. Let the children cut their own flower shapes.

2. Cut flower shapes from wrapping paper or wallpaper.

3. Omit the faces. Instead write the children's names inside the flowers.

Loved by the Lord

BIBLE STORY

The Parable of the Lost Sheep
(Luke 15:1–7)

MATERIALS

White, green, and blue poster paper
Scissors
Cotton balls
White pipe cleaners
Craft glue

TEACHER TASKS

1. Cover the top third of the bulletin board with blue poster paper.

2. Cut green poster paper to cover the bottom two-thirds of the bulletin board. Curve the top to represent a hillside. Place it on a work table.

3. Cut letters from white poster paper for the words "Loved by the Lord." Attach them to the top of the bulletin board.

4. Cut white pipe cleaners into segments that can be twisted around a cotton ball.

5. Set out cotton balls and glue.

6. Read Luke 15:1–7. Emphasize that Jesus is the Good Shepherd. He knows us and we know Him.

7. Attach the green poster paper to the bulletin board. Make a pipe-cleaner shepherd and attach it to the bulletin board.

STUDENT TASKS

1. Wrap two pipe cleaners around a cotton ball to make a lamb.

2. Glue your lamb to the paper.

OTHER IDEAS

1. Let the students write their name by their lamb.

2. Have the children make 100 sheep to put on the board. Place one sheep away from the rest. Ask a child to draw a picture of the Good Shepherd looking for His sheep. Add it to the bulletin board.

3. Glue movable eyes onto each sheep.

4. Glue the sheep to green poster board.

Jesus the Good Shepherd

BIBLE STORY

The Shepherd and His Flock
(John 10:1–18)

MATERIALS

Green or blue fabric
White paper
Scissors
White poster board
Marker
White cotton balls
Craft glue
Gold yarn

TEACHER TASKS

1. Cover the top half of the bulletin board with blue fabric. Cover the bottom half with green fabric.

2. Cut letters from white paper for the words "Jesus the Good Shepherd." Attach them to the bulletin board.

3. Enlarge the pattern on page 45 and trace it directly onto white poster board. Cut it out. Draw in the ear, eye, and mouth with a marker. Place the sheep on a work table.

4. Cut yarn into 18" pieces.

5. Set out cotton balls, glue, scissors, and yarn.

6. Read John 10:11–14. Ask the children how God takes care of them.

7. Attach the sheep and the staff to the bulletin board.

STUDENT TASKS

1. Glue cotton balls onto the sheep.

2. Glue pieces of yarn onto the staff.

3. Tell one way God takes care of you.

OTHER IDEAS

1. Use blue and green poster paper for the background.

2. Cut sheep from felt or another fabric.

Pattern for "Jesus the Good Shepherd"

Jesus Listens when I Pray

BIBLE STORY

Jesus Shows Us How to Pray
(Matthew 6:5–15)

MATERIALS

> Print fabric
> Solid-colored fabric
> Pinking shears
> Markers
> Pencil

TEACHER TASKS

1. Cover the bulletin board with print fabric.

2. With the pinking shears, cut a square of the solid-colored fabric for each child. Cut one extra square.

3. Write "Jesus Listens when I Pray" on the extra fabric square. Attach it to the middle of the bulletin board.

4. Remind the children that Jesus promises to hear us when we pray.

5. Help young children trace their hands on the fabric.

6. Arrange the fabric squares to make a quilt design on the bulletin board.

STUDENT TASKS

1. Use a pencil to trace your hand, fingers together, on a fabric square.

2. Trace over the pencil line with a marker. Write your name inside your handprint.

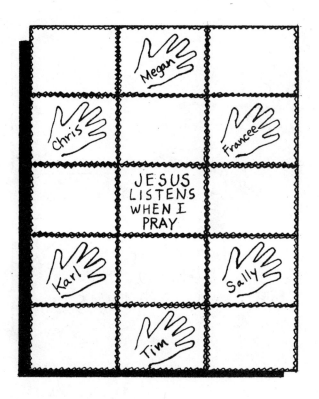

OTHER IDEAS

1. Draw the hands and names on a single piece of solid-colored fabric.

2. Cover the bulletin board with patterned wrapping paper. Cut squares from solid-colored wrapping paper.

3. Use colored glue or fabric paint to draw the handprints and names.

4. Sew the pieces of fabric together to make a patchwork wall hanging or banner.

5. Write all or part of the Lord's Prayer on the center patch.

God's Loving Children

BIBLE STORY

The Good Samaritan (Luke 10:25–37)

MATERIALS

Heart-patterned wrapping paper
Red and white construction paper
Scissors
Glue
Markers or crayons
Black, brown, yellow, and red yarn

TEACHER TASKS

1. Cover the bulletin board with heart-patterned wrapping paper.

2. Cut letters from construction paper for the words "God's Loving Children." Attach them to the bulletin board.

3. Cut large hearts from red construction paper and smaller hearts from white construction paper for each child. Use the patterns on page 48 if needed.

4. Cut yarn into 6" to 8" pieces.

5. Set out glue, markers, and scissors.

6. Attach the heart portraits to the bulletin board.

STUDENT TASKS

1. Glue the white heart inside the red heart.

2. Use markers or crayons to make the white heart into a self-portrait.

3. Glue on yarn for hair. Trim as needed.

OTHER IDEAS

1. Cut strips of paper. Accordion-fold the strips to make pop-up arms and legs. Add a smaller heart for the head and use the other hearts as the body.

2. Use cut pieces of construction paper to add facial details.

3. Adapt this bulletin board for other lessons that emphasize the love God wants His children to show others.

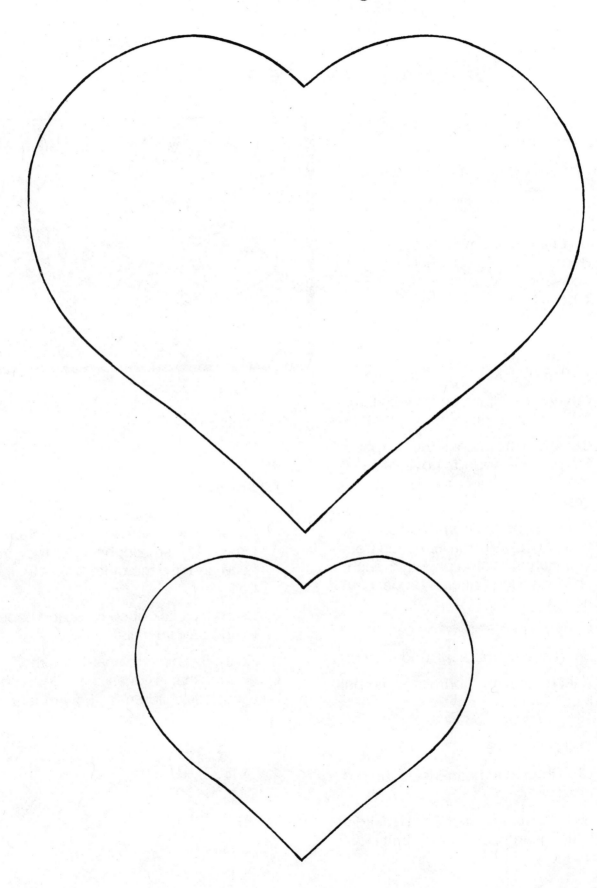

Ways God Helps

BIBLE STORY

Jesus Heals an Official's Son
(John 4:43–54)

MATERIALS

White poster paper
Construction paper
Scissors
White crayon
Toy medical kit
Simple first-aid objects (adhesive
    bandages, gauze pads, first-aid
    tape, etc.)
Pencil
Glue

TEACHER TASKS

1. Cut white poster paper to cover the bulletin board. Place it on a work table.

2. Cut letters from construction paper for the words "Ways God Helps." Attach them to the poster paper.

3. Draw a praying hands and a Bible on construction paper. Cut them out and use a white crayon to write "Holy-Bible" on the Bible shape. Attach them to the center of the poster paper.

4. Set out toy medical equipment and first–aid supplies, construction paper, pencils, glue, and scissors.

5. Explain that God has given us many things to help us when we are sick. Show the medical equipment. Emphasize that God has also given us prayer and His Word so that we can ask Him for help and hear His words of promise.

6. Attach the poster paper to the bulletin board.

STUDENT TASKS

1. Pick a toy medical tool or first-aid object to trace on construction paper. Cut it out.

2. Glue your tool or object onto the poster paper.

OTHER IDEAS

1. Draw a medical bag on the poster paper. Have the children put the medical tools inside the bag.

2. Have the children draw the medical tools instead of trace them. Add details with markers or crayons.

3. Attach lightweight first-aid objects to the bulletin board.

Thank the Lord

BIBLE STORY

The Feeding of the Five Thousand
(Mark 6:30–44)

MATERIALS

Colorful poster paper
Food advertising pages from the
    newspaper
Scissors
Paper bag
Glue
Food labels and box tops
Stick pins

TEACHER TASKS

1. Cover the bulletin board with poster paper.

2. Cut letters from the food advertising pages for the words "Thank the Lord." Attach them to the bulletin board.

3. Cut letters from the food advertising pages for the words "For All His Gifts." Glue them to the plain side of a paper bag. Use stick pins to attach the bag to the bulletin board.

4. Set out labels, boxes, food advertising pages, scissors, and glue.

5. Tell the children that before He fed the 5,000, Jesus blessed the food. Emphasize that we should thank God for the food He has given us.

6. Use stick pins to fasten lightweight food boxes to the bulletin board.

STUDENT TASKS

1. Cut and glue pictures of food to the bulletin board.

2. Trim food labels and glue them to the bulletin board.

3. Place extra food labels, pictures, and lightweight boxes inside the grocery bag.

4. Take turns pulling out a label, picture, or box from the bag. Say a thank-You prayer for the food it represents.

OTHER IDEAS

1. Glue the paper bag flat onto the board.

2. Cut a cornucopia. Fill it with food pictures and labels.

3. Cover the bulletin board with food advertising pages. Cut the letters from white construction paper.

Jesus' Life of Love

BIBLE STORIES

The Miracles of Jesus (The Four Gospels)

MATERIALS

Wallpaper
Construction paper
Scissors
Drawing paper
Box lids
Markers, crayons, or colored pencils
Glue
Push pins

TEACHER TASKS

1. Cover the bulletin board with wallpaper.

2. Cut letters from construction paper for the words "Jesus' Life of Love." Attach them to the bulletin board.

3. Cut a piece of drawing paper to fit inside each box lid. Have one box lid for each child.

4. Set out markers, crayons, or colored pencils, and glue.

5. Ask the children to name and discuss some of the miracles Jesus did. Have them select a miracle and illustrate it.

6. Use stick pins to attach the box lids to the bulletin board.

STUDENT TASKS

1. Draw a picture of one of Jesus' miracles.

2. Glue the picture inside the box lid.

3. Tell about the miracle you pictured.

OTHER IDEAS

1. Glue pictures from Bible-story leaflets inside the box lids.

2. Write the name of the miracle shown in the picture below the box lid.

3. Use torn pieces of construction paper to make the pictures.

4. Decorate the outside of the lid with rickrack, ribbon, yarn, markers, or paper.

Praise to the King

BIBLE STORY

Jesus Enters Jerusalem
(Matthew 21:1–11)

MATERIALS

Yellow poster paper
Green plastic tape
Waxed paper
Scissors

TEACHER TASKS

1. Cut yellow poster paper to cover the bulletin board. Place it on a work table.

2. Make the words "Praise to the King" on the poster paper with green plastic tape.

3. Cut a rectangle of waxed paper for each child.

4. Cut one long strip and several smaller pieces of green tape for each child. Place the tape on the waxed paper.

5. Describe the sight of Jesus' entry into Jerusalem. Emphasize that the people laid the palm branches and clothing along the road to worship Jesus as their King.

6. Attach the yellow poster paper to the bulletin board.

STUDENT TASKS

1. Stick the long piece of green tape on the yellow poster paper.

2. Stick the smaller pieces of tape along the center strip to make leaves (fronds).

OTHER IDEAS

1. Use green self-adhesive ribbon or strips of green construction paper to make the palm leaves instead of green tape.

2. Add the words of a praise song familiar to the children to the bulletin board. Sing the song during your worship.

Hosanna

BIBLE STORY

Children Praise Jesus in the Temple
(Matthew 21:14–16)

MATERIALS

Yellow poster paper
Construction paper
Scissors
Glitter pen
Brightly colored stickers

TEACHER TASKS

1. Cover the bulletin board with yellow poster paper.

2. Cut large letters from construction paper for the word *Hosanna.*

3. Set out glitter pens and stickers.

4. Tell the children that *hosanna* means "Save, we pray." Emphasize that the children were praising Jesus as their Savior and we should too.

5. Attach the letters to the bulletin board.

STUDENT TASKS

1. Work in groups to decorate each letter with glitter pens and stickers.

2. Add stickers to the yellow poster paper.

OTHER IDEAS

1. Cut the letters from poster board and use craft glue to glue on sequins and metallic trim.

2. Glue pieces of metallic or neon construction paper on the letters.

3. Cut the letters for the words "Hosanna to the King."

4. Trace the letters on the poster paper. Fill them in with hole-punched circles or small pieces of paper.

5. Cut the letters from wrapping paper.

6. Decorate the letters and background with yarn, colored glue, or glitter.

7. Spatter or spray bright tempera paint over the letters.

Signs of God's Love

BIBLE STORY

The Lord's Supper (Matthew 26:17–30)

MATERIALS

> Purple fabric
> White poster paper
> Scissors
> Gold and silver metallic wrapping
>   paper
> Glue

TEACHER TASKS

1. Cover the bulletin board with purple fabric.

2. Cut letters from white poster paper for the words "Signs of God's Love." Attach them to the bulletin board.

3. Enlarge the patterns on page 55 and trace them directly onto white poster paper. Cut them out.

4. Cut metallic wrapping paper into 1" squares.

5. Set out glue.

6. Tell the children about the "new covenant" Jesus instituted on Maundy Thursday. Emphasize that it is a sign of God's love and forgiveness that He gives us through Jesus' death and resurrection.

7. Attach the cup to the bulletin board. Place the circle on top of the cup's top edge.

STUDENT TASKS

1. Glue gold squares to fill in the cup.

2. Glue silver squares to fill in the circle.

OTHER IDEAS

1. Cover the cup and circle with cut or torn pieces of construction paper.

2. Instead of a circle, use the outline of a piece of bread.

3. Add a baptismal font to the picture.

Patterns for "Signs of God's Love"

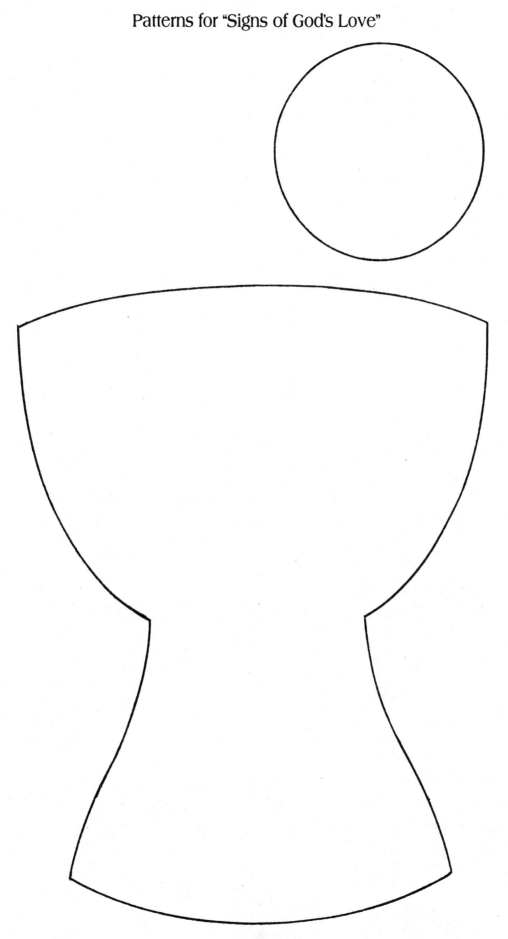

See How God Loved

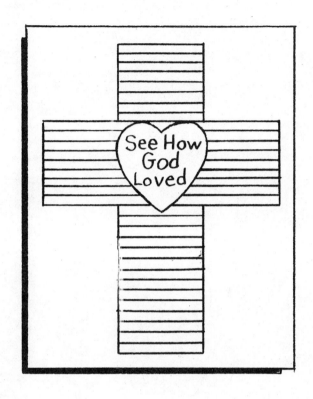

BIBLE STORY

Jesus' Death (Matthew 27:32–54)

MATERIALS

Purple poster paper
Red construction paper
Scissors
Markers
Brown plastic tape
Waxed paper

TEACHER TASKS

1. Cut purple poster paper to cover the bulletin board. Place it on a work table.

2. Fold a piece of red construction paper in half. Draw half a heart along the fold and cut it out.

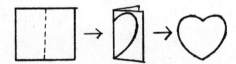

3. Write "See How God Loved" on the heart.

4. Outline a cross shape with brown plastic tape in the center of the poster paper.

5. Cut squares of waxed paper.

6. Cut the brown plastic tape into 4" to 5" pieces. Stick them to the waxed paper.

7. Attach the poster paper to the bulletin board. Attach the heart in the center.

STUDENT TASK

Work together to tape the brown plastic tape inside the cross outline.

OTHER IDEAS

1. Fill in the cross shape with pieces cut or torn from paper bags.

2. Draw a ___ r around the cross. Cover i ___ pieces of cut or torn constru ___ paper.

3. Cover t ___ ss with cut-out flowers or brigh ___ red paper to make an Easter ___

Alleluia

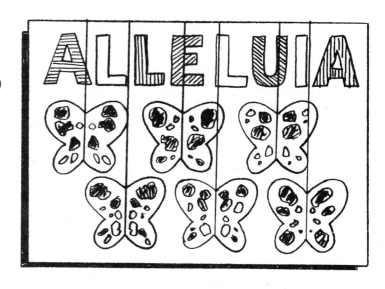

BIBLE STORY

Jesus' Resurrection (Matthew 28:1–10)

MATERIALS

> Blue poster paper
> Construction paper
> Scissors
> Pencil
> Tempera paint
> Paintbrush
> Yarn
> Glue

TEACHER TASKS

1. Cover the bulletin board with blue poster paper.

2. Cut letters from construction paper for the word *Alleluia.* Attach them to the bulletin board.

3. Duplicate the pattern on page 58 for each child.

4. Set out construction paper, tempera paint, paintbrushes, scissors, and pieces of yarn.

5. Describe how a butterfly comes out of a dead-looking cocoon. Explain that the butterfly is a symbol of Jesus' resurrection and of our new life in Christ.

6. Use yarn to hang the butterflies from the top of the bulletin board.

STUDENT TASKS

1. Fold construction paper in half. Use the pattern to trace a butterfly along the fold or draw half a butterfly along the fold. Cut it out. Unfold.

2. Use the paintbrush to dot tempera paint inside the butterfly. Fold, press down, and open to dry.

3. Glue one end of a piece of yarn down the center of the butterfly. Let dry.

OTHER IDEAS

1. Cut the butterflies and letters from metallic or decorative paper.

2. Omit tempera paint. Decorate the butterflies with sequins or colorful self-adhesive circles.

3. Write the word *Alleluia* across the butterflies. Fold them in the middle, decorate, and glue on the bulletin board.

4. Omit the yarn. Attach the butterflies to the bulletin board.

5. Sprinkle glitter on the wet tempera paint.

Pattern for "Alleluia"

I Can Tell

BIBLE STORY

The Great Commission
(Matthew 28:16–20)

MATERIALS

Poster paper
Flesh-colored construction paper
Scissors
Crayons or fine-point markers
Yarn

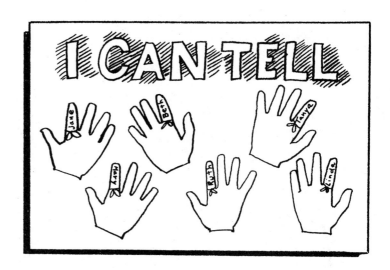

TEACHER TASKS

1. Cover the bulletin board with poster paper.

2. Cut letters from construction paper for the words "I Can Tell." Attach them to the bulletin board.

3. Cut a 5″ piece of yarn for each child.

4. Set out construction paper, scissors, and crayons or fine-point markers.

5. Help young children trace and cut out their handprints. Help them tie the piece of yarn around one finger.

6. Read Matthew 28:19–20. Emphasize that we can tell others about Jesus too. Explain that sometimes people tie a string around their finger to remind them of something important. It's important to remember to tell others about Jesus.

7. Attach the handprints to the bulletin board.

STUDENT TASKS

1. Trace your hand with your fingers spread out on construction paper. Cut it out.

2. Write the name of the person you want to tell about Jesus on the hand.

3. Tie a piece of yarn around the first finger.

OTHER IDEAS

1. Outline the children's hands directly on the poster paper. Glue a bow on the finger.

2. Omit the yarn. Draw a picture on each finger of someone to tell about Jesus.

God Goes with Us

BIBLE STORY

Life of Paul (Acts 9:1–31; 13:1–28:31)

MATERIALS

Map
Construction paper
Scissors
White poster paper
Fine-point markers

TEACHER TASKS

1. Cover the bulletin board with a map or several maps.

2. Cut letters from construction paper for the words "God Goes with Us." Attach them to the bulletin board.

3. Cut white poster paper into postcard-size pieces.

4. Set out fine-point markers.

5. Talk about how God took care of Paul on his missionary journeys. Discuss how God takes care of us in all of our travels. Ask the children to choose a place they have visited to draw on a postcard.

6. Attach the postcards to the bulletin board.

STUDENT TASKS

1. Draw a picture postcard of a place you have visited.

2. Thank God for keeping you safe on your trip.

OTHER IDEAS

1. Have children bring real postcards to put on the map.

2. For older children who can write, ask them to write a prayer on the postcard thanking God for His care during their trip.

3. Use crayons instead of markers.

4. Go on a class trip. Take pictures of the children on the trip to put on the bulletin board.

Alphabet Letters

Enlarge the letters to fit the bulletin board design you are making.

1. Trace the letters on a piece of acetate.

2. Use an overhead projector to project the letters on poster paper or poster board taped to the wall.

3. Trace the letters on the paper or poster board. Cut out and use as patterns.

AaBbCcDd
EeFfGgHhIiJj
KkLlMmNnOo
PpQqRrSsTt
UuVvWwXxYyZz
1234567890
(!?,. " ")

A a B b C c D d E e
F f G g H h I i J j
K k L l M m N n
O o P p Q q R r
S s T t U u V v
W w X x Y y Z z
1 2 3 4 5 6 7
8 9 0 (! ? , . " ")